HOW TO IMPROVE AT SWIMMING

All the information you need to know to get on top of your game!

W9-AHF-487

More than just instructional guides, the **HOW TO IMPROVE AT...** series gives you everything you need to achieve your goals—tips on technique, step-by-step demonstrations, nutritional advice, and the secrets of successful pro athletes. Excellent visual instructions and expert advice combine to act as your own personal trainer. These books aim to give you the know-how and confidence to improve your performance.

Studies have shown that an active approach to life makes you feel happier and less stressed. The easiest way to start is by taking up a new sport or improving your skills in an existing one. You simply have to choose an activity that enthuses you.

HOW TO IMPROVE AT SWIMMING does not promise instant success. It simply gives you the tools to become the best at whatever you choose to do.

Every care has been taken to ensure that these instructions are safe to follow, but in the event of injury Crabtree Publishing shall not be liable for any injuries or damages.

By Paul Mason

Crabtree Publishing Company
www.crabtreebooks.com

Cover: Swimming star Katie Hoff
Special thank you to: Elizabeth Wiggans for her assistance
Photography: Roddy Paine Photographic Studios
Illustrations: John Alston

Photo credits: Associated Press: front cover; Empics: p. 36 middle, center and bottom, p. 37, top and center, p. 38 top, center and bottom, p. 39 center and bottom, p. 40 center, p. 41 top and bottom, p. 42 top and center; Corbis: p. 40 top, p. 41 center, p. 42 bottom, p. 43 bottom, p. 47 top, p. 45 bottom.

Library and Archives Canada Cataloguing in Publication

Mason, Paul, 1967-
    How to improve at swimming / Paul Mason.

(How to improve at...)
Includes index.
ISBN 978-0-7787-3570-0 (bound).--ISBN 978-0-7787-3592-2 (pbk.)

    1. Swimming--Training--Juvenile literature. I. Title. II. Series.

GV837.6.M38 2007   j797.2'1   C2007-904703-3

Library of Congress Cataloging-in-Publication Data

Mason, Paul, 1967-
    How to improve at swimming / Paul Mason.
        p. cm. -- (How to improve at--)
    Includes index.
    ISBN-13: 978-0-7787-3570-0 (rlb)
    ISBN-10: 0-7787-3570-2 (rlb)
    ISBN-13: 978-0-7787-3592-2 (pb)
    ISBN-10: 0-7787-3592-3 (pb)
    1. Swimming for children--Training--Juvenile literature. I. Title. II. Series.

    GV837.2.M374 2008
    797.2'1083--dc22   2007030346

Crabtree Publishing Company
www.crabtreebooks.com   1-800-387-7650

Published in Canada
Crabtree Publishing
616 Welland Ave.
St. Catharines, Ontario
L2M 5V6

Published in the United States
Crabtree Publishing
PMB16A
350 Fifth Ave., Suite 3308
New York, NY 10118

Published by CRABTREE PUBLISHING COMPANY
Copyright © **2008**

CONTENTS

● **STARTS AND TURNS**

LEARNING TO DIVE	26-27
RACING STARTS	28-29
RACING TURNS	30-31
BACKSTROKE STARTS AND TURNS	32-33

● **BE FIT, STAY FIT**

DIET AND FITNESS	34-35

● **RACE TACTICS & EVENTS**

RACE TACTICS & EVENTS	36-37

● **SWIMMING IN OTHER SPORTS**

SWIMMING IN OTHER SPORTS	38-39
TRIATHLON & WATER POLO	40-41

● **SAFETY**

WATER SAFETY	42-43
LIFESAVING	44-45

● **HOW THE PROS DO IT** 44-45

● **GLOSSARY & INDEX** 48

● **INTRODUCTION** 3

● **KNOW THE SPORT**

SWIMMING POOLS	4-5
EQUIPMENT	6-7

● **THE STROKES**

WARMING UP	8-9
FREESTYLE	10-13
BACKSTROKE	14-17
BREASTSTROKE	18-21
BASIC BUTTERFLY	22-23
ADVANCED BUTTERFLY	24-25

INTRODUCTION

There are plenty of reasons to want to improve your swimming skills. Some people swim as a way to keep fit. Other people want to join swimming teams. Maybe you want to learn to play water polo, ride the waves on a surf board, or even train as a lifeguard! But the best reason for learning to swim well is that it makes it more fun.

GUIDE TO TERMS

To help you understand the terms in this book, we have used the following:

"Arm stroke"   *the arm action that moves you through the water.*

"Leg kick"   *the action of your legs that moves you through the water.*

"Pull"   *the part of your arm stroke that moves you farther.*

"Overarm recovery"   *the part of the swimming stroke that takes place above water.*

SWIMMING POOLS

*T*here are lots of places where you can go swimming. Most people swim in swimming pools. Sometimes pools are set up for racing, with separate lanes, diving blocks, and other equipment. Wherever you go, be sure that there's a lifeguard on duty.

LANE LINES

These divide the pool into lanes. They float on the surface and help make sure that the racers swim in a straight line. In most pools, these lane lines have special floats on them that stop waves from going from one lane to another. These are called "anti-turbulence lines".

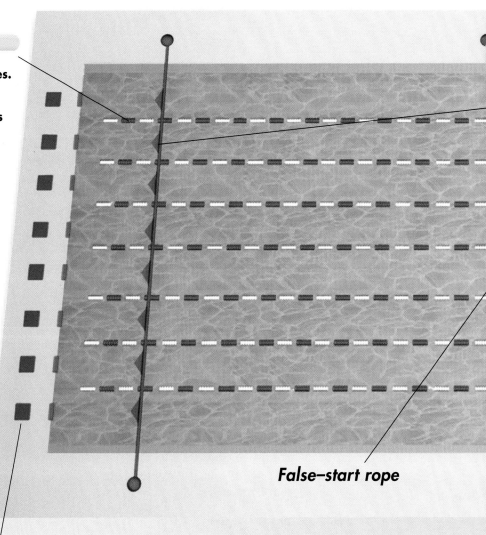

False–start rope

STARTING BLOCKS

These let the racers get a faster start. For freestyle, butterfly, and breaststroke, the swimmers dive off of these starting blocks. In backstroke races, swimmers hang on to them while in the water.

This allows the starter to stop the swimmers if one of them has dived in too soon. If there is a false start, the rope is dropped into the water, and the swimmers swim into it. They know then that they have to go back and start again.

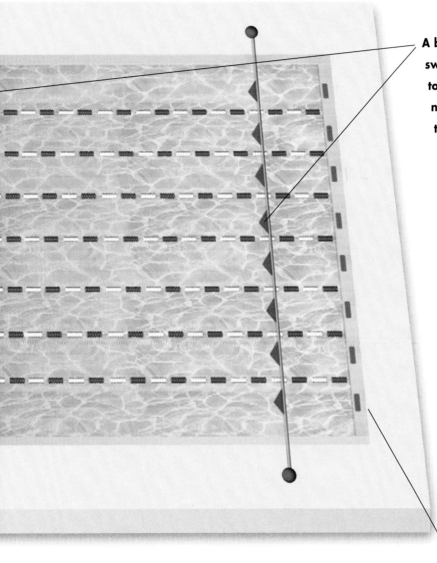

A backstroke flag tells backstroke swimmers when they are getting close to the wall. The swimmers count the number of strokes that it takes them to get from the flag to the wall. The next time that they swim under the flag, they won't need to look around to see how close the wall is.

When the starter fires the start gun, the clock begins to run. Each lane has a special pad at the end that stops the clock when the swimmer's hand touches it at the end of the race. The swimmer's time then appears on a large screen at the side of the pool.

*S*wimming is a simple sport that does not need much equipment. However, there are several things that you can buy to help you improve your swimming. Some of the best items are floats that you can use for practice using your legs or arms only. These help you to practice specific parts of your stroke.

SWIMSUIT

Swimmers wear one-piece swimsuits. These are tight fitting to allow the swimmer to move through the water more smoothly. Some swimmers wear special "sharkskin" suits for racing. A raised texture on the surface of the material improves the flow of water along the body. This texture makes the swimsuit more streamlined.

SWIMMING CAP

If you have long hair, it's best to wrap it up in a swimming cap to prevent it from getting in your eyes. Caps also protect your hair from chlorine and make you more streamlined.

GOGGLES

These stop your eyes from getting sore and help you see where you are going under water. It's important that your goggles fit well. Try on different goggles before deciding which kind fits you best.

TOWEL

Don't forget your towel! If you're going to be getting in and out of the water and drying yourself off between swims, it's best to take two towels. Save one so that you have a dry towel ready at the end of your swim.

KICKBOARD

These are used for swimming with your legs only, which is a good way to practice your kicking. Place the board under your hands to support your upper body.

PULL BUOY

There are several types of pull buoys. These are used for arm exercises. Place the buoy between your thighs so that you can focus on your arms.

CHECKLIST

- Two towels.
- Tracksuit and t-shirt for keeping warm.
- Spare swimsuit and goggles for emergencies. (Take the spare goggles up to the start in case your favorite ones break as you put them on.)
- Swimming cap.
- Bag to hold everything.

WARMING UP

Before you start a swimming practice, it's a good idea to do some warm-up exercises. Warming up helps you avoid straining your muscles and makes an injury less likely. For swimmers, the warm up should be in two parts: first do some exercises on the land, then do some gentle swimming before you start your practice.

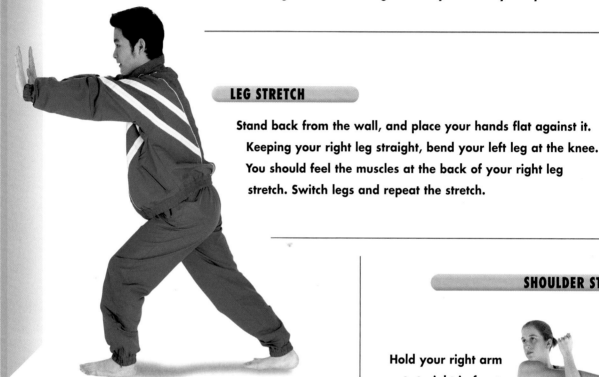

LEG STRETCH

Stand back from the wall, and place your hands flat against it. Keeping your right leg straight, bend your left leg at the knee. You should feel the muscles at the back of your right leg stretch. Switch legs and repeat the stretch.

SHOULDER STRETCH

Hold your right arm out straight in front of you. Pull it across the front of your body, and use the inside of your left elbow to hold it in place. Repeat with your left arm.

PELICAN THIGH STRETCH

Stand with your feet flat on the floor. Lift one leg, and hold the foot behind you with both hands. Now gently pull your heel toward your buttocks. It's important to keep your hips level while you do this exercise. Don't arch your back to try to get your foot up farther! Repeat with the other leg.

TOP TIP

Whenever you are warming up, take care not to stretch your muscles too far. You should stretch only until you feel a slight tightness, and then stop.

SIDE STRETCH

Stand with your feet a little more than shoulder width apart. Keep your body relaxed, and lean to the left. Try to make an arc with your body and right arm. Lean as far as you can without straining. Repeat the stretch to the other side.

ARM STRETCH

Reach your left arm behind your head, pointing down the line of your spine. Now reach your right arm up your back along your spine, and try to touch your hands together. Reverse your arms and repeat the stretch.

FULL BODY STRETCH

Crouch down low with your heels flat on the floor and your arms out in front of you. Stand up slowly and bring your hands up in front of your body until you are standing on your tiptoes with your arms stretching up to the ceiling. Inhale as you go up and hold the stretch for a few seconds. Exhale as you return to a standing position. Try doing this stretch underneath a ceiling that you can just reach on your tiptoes. Touching the ceiling will help you hold the stretch position.

FREESTYLE

Freestyle is the stroke that most swimmers use if they are training for competitions or to get fit. It is the fastest of the four strokes, so you can swim farther in an hour doing freestyle than you would doing breaststroke. This stroke is also known as the front crawl.

LEARNING TO BREATHE

The secret to breathing while swimming is to inhale when your face is out of water and exhale when you are underwater. For freestyle, you breathe by lifting your face to the side. Here is a practice exercise to help you learn freestyle breathing. Practice breathing on both sides if you can.

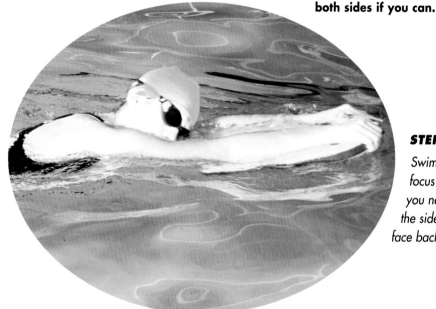

STEP 1

Swim along using a kickboard as you focus on your breathing. As soon as you need a breath, turn your head to the side. Take a breath and put your face back under water.

STEP 2

You can breathe out all at once, using the "explosive" method, or gradually, using the "trickle" method.

FREESTYLE RHYTHM

STEP 1

After you have pushed off from the wall, pull your left arm underneath your body, leaving the right straight out in front. As your left arm reaches the end of its underwater stroke, lift it out of the water. Kick both legs to propel you forward.

STEP 2

As the left arm starts to come through the air, your right arm pulls under your body. As your right arm "pulls" through the water, it propels your body forward and keeps you afloat.

STEP 3

The stroke continues back and forth between your left and right arms. Keep your legs moving by kicking your feet up and down from your hips as well as your knees.

In all strokes, your hands should be cupped to "catch" the water.

ARM MOVEMENT

STEP 1

Extend one arm fully in front of you, and feel the stretch as it enters the water. Note the tilt of your body as your other arm lifts out of the water.

STEP 2

As you pull back under water, bend your arm at the elbow so that your hand is in line with the center line of your body.

center line

TOP TIP

Imagine a center line that runs from your head to the tips of your toes. Use this line to align your arms and legs correctly for the stroke.

FREESTYLE
CONTINUED

Once you have learned the basic freestyle stroke, you can start to work on your arm movement. Even good swimmers can sometimes make big improvements in two main areas: the underwater stroke and the overarm recovery.

UNDERWATER STROKE

The underwater stroke is where most of your speed comes from, so it's important for this stroke to be as powerful and effective as possible.

STEP 1
Your right arm enters the water straight ahead of you. Before you start to pull your arm back, let your shoulder drop forward slightly.

STEP 2
Pull your arm slightly away from your imaginary center line.

STEP 3
Your hand can cross the center line a little, underneath your body. The arm performs an "S" shape movement as it moves under you.

STEP 4
Now pull your arm back toward your hip. As your hand leaves the water, your other hand should just be entering it.

The overarm recovery helps keep your stroke smooth and your body balanced.

STEP 1

Lift your right arm out of the water with the elbow bent. Your left arm should just be starting its underwater stroke.

STEP 2

Continue to bring your hand forward, and lift your elbow slightly.

STEP 3

As your elbow reaches its highest point, your hand should be just reaching your shoulder.

STEP 4

As your hand moves in front of your shoulder, drop your elbow, and start to stretch out your arm. Your left arm is now halfway through its underwater stroke.

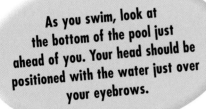

As you swim, look at the bottom of the pool just ahead of you. Your head should be positioned with the water just over your eyebrows.

STEP 5

Slide your hand into the water. Your other arm should just be coming out of the water.

TOP TIP

When you are doing your underwater stroke, don't rush. Instead try to "feel" the water, catching it in your cupped hands. Imagine that you are pulling a "chunk" of water toward you and moving over it.

BACKSTROKE

Backstroke is swum while looking up at the roof or sky. People often confuse backstroke with an upside-down freestyle stroke. One of the most important secrets of swimming the backstroke well is to keep your head and body as still as possible.

BACKSTROKE RHYTHM

People learning the backstroke sometimes move their arms too deeply into the water. The underwater pull for the backstroke goes to the side of the body, not underneath it. Your arms only need to be deep enough to be sure that your hands won't break the surface in the middle of your pull.

STEP 1
With your right arm at full stretch, your left arm should be just about to come out of the water.

STEP 2
Your right arm pulls down through the water as your left arm comes through the air.

STEP 3
Your right hand is just below the surface during the middle of your stroke.

STEP 4
Just as your right arm gets to the end of its stroke, your left arm is about to enter the water above your head.

As your arms propel you through the water, keep your hips high and your body straight.

STEP 1

When an arm enters the water, it goes in straight, with the little finger of your cupped hand pointing downward into the water. The palm faces away from you.

STEP 2

When an arm has finished its pull, it comes straight up through the air. Kick hard continuously to keep your body flat in the water.

Your hand should go in with the little finger first. This puts your hand in the right position to start the underwater pull stroke.

Your arms should be straight as they go through the air. They only bend after they have entered the water.

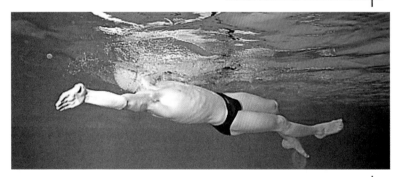

TOP TIP

Try to establish a breathing rhythm that is in time with your stroke action.

BACKSTROKE
CONTINUED

Asmooth, steady kick is very important for backstroke swimmers. If your kick is weak, your hips and legs will sink down. This body position means that your arms have to work harder to drag your body through the water. A powerful kick keeps your lower body up high and allows you to swim smoothly.

UNDERWATER STROKE

Having a smooth, powerful underwater stroke helps you keep your head straight in the water, which allows you to swim faster. As in freestyle, try to keep your body straight. Think about your imaginary center line. Twisting from side to side will slow you down.

The head is in line with the body.

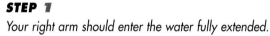

STEP 1

Your right arm should enter the water fully extended.

STEP 2

As your left arm rises out of the water, your right arm starts to sweep to the side.

The arm pulls through the water at an angle.

The arm is at a 90° angle.

STEP 3

Move the right arm so that it is halfway through the stroke and at 90° to your body.

The open hand acts as a paddle.

STEP 4

As your arm comes out of the underwater stroke, the palm faces toward the hip.

This arm enters ...

...as the other one exits.

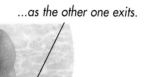

STEP 5

As your left arm goes back into the water, your right arm starts to come out. Your legs should feel long and stretched and your ankles should feel loose as you kick.

TOP TIP

Keep looking straight up at the ceiling. If you find yourself looking back where you've just come from, you know that your body is in the wrong position in the water.

BREASTSTROKE

The breaststroke is often the first stroke that people can do when they learn to swim. It feels comfortable because it lets you swim with your face out of the water. The breaststroke can also be an extremely fast stroke if you can get the right rhythm between your arms and legs.

BREASTSTROKE RHYTHM

One of the most important things to learn for the breaststroke is when to put your face into the water. The stroke's rhythm and speed come from the balance between swimming under water and rising above it.

STEP 1
Start your stroke by moving your arms out and back in a circular motion. Your legs should be trailing behind you.

STEP 2
As you pull your arms in, your body rises up, and your legs come back toward your bottom. Breathe in.

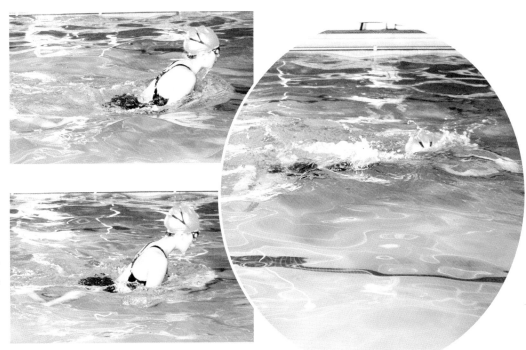

STEP 3
As your hands start to move forward again, your legs extend out behind you ready for the next kick.

STEP 4
Your body drops back down into the water.

STEP 5
Bring your legs forward and your feet to your buttocks. Kick backward and glide (see top right). You are now ready to repeat the stroke.

GLIDING

After your kick, let yourself glide forward with your arms and legs stretched out. Just before you start to slow down, begin your next arm stroke.

BODY POSITION

As your hands come back in close to your body, your head lifts up, and your legs start to get into position for the next kick.

TOP TIP

Always try to begin your kick with your heels close to (or even touching) your bottom. End your kick with your toes pointing back and your feet together.

BREASTSTROKE CONTINUED

There are two main ways of doing a breaststroke pull. Some swimmers let their arms glide forward and keep them nearly straight until they are ready to pull them back to lift up their bodies. Other swimmers bend their arms almost immediately, so they seem to be pulling back more. Try both ways to find the one that suits you best.

HAND MOVEMENT

Finding the right time to pull your hands back through the water is very important if you want to swim faster. Some swimmers find that the best moment to sweep their hands in after the glide is at the moment when they can't see them through their goggles anymore.

STEP 1
As you glide forward, your hands are together with the little finger highest.

STEP 2
Your hands sweep out, keeping up your speed from the glide.

STEP 3
Finally, your hands sweep in, as you bring your legs up, ready for the next kick.

Most of your speed in the breaststroke comes from your legs. Although your arms drive you forward, their main job is to get your body into position for the next leg kick.

STEP 1

After your kick, let yourself glide forward with your arms and legs outstretched.

STEP 2

Just before you start to slow down, begin your next arm and leg strokes.

STEP 3

As your arms begin to move back, your legs move forward, with the knees leading.

STEP 4

Continue to bring your legs forward, while your arms complete the circular motion to return to the starting position. Keep your feet flat and facing out so that they act as "paddles" when you kick backward.

TOP TIP

It is important to get the timing of your kick and pull right. You should be gliding forward after your kick, then use your arm stroke to lift your body up, ready for the next big kick.

BASIC BUTTERFLY

When you first start learning to swim the butterfly, it is very important to get the proper body position. The most common problem is letting your body sink too low in the water. When your hips sink, your arms have to do more work. Your elbows drag in the water during your overarm stroke, and it's harder to rise up and take a breath.

BUTTERFLY RYTHYM

The underwater stroke for the butterfly is basically the same as for freestyle (see pages 12–13), except that your arms and legs do the same thing at the same time. The movement most people find difficult is the two-arm recovery.

STEP 1

At the end of your pull, your body comes high up out of the water. Your arms come out and start to swing forward.

STEP 2

As your arms swing toward the front of your body, your head starts to drop down into the water.

STEP 3

Your face will just be going under. Your next pull is what lifts your head up again.

DOLPHIN KICK

To do a dolphin kick, your feet and legs must be together. Your hips then move up and down and send a wave-like movement down your legs to your feet. The golden rule is to do one full kick as your arms enter the water and one as they come out of it.

Getting the arm movement correct is essential to time your breathing correctly.

STEP 1

Move your arms into the water together, about shoulder width apart. They are now ready for the pull.

STEP 2

As you pull back, bend your arms slightly so that your hands go under your body.

STEP 3

During the overarm recovery, you can either lift your head to take a breath or keep your head down. Many swimmers take one breath every two full arm strokes.

TOP TIP

When you start learning the butterfly, breathe with every arm stroke. Once you feel a little more confident, try breathing every two or three strokes.

ADVANCED BUTTERFLY

Once you start swimming the butterfly faster, your stroke needs to change from when you were learning. Beginners do the butterfly as an up-and-down stroke, with their heads and shoulders coming a long way out of the water. The fastest butterfly swimmers concentrate on moving forward, not up and down.

TWO-ARM RECOVERY

One of the keys to swimming a fast butterfly is how you breathe. Your head and shoulders should be in the same position the whole time, whether you are taking a breath or not. To breathe, you simply lift your chin and take a breath before dropping it back down.

STEP 1

As your arms come out of the water, push your chin forward and take a breath. Your shoulders should stay quite low (compare this photo with the one on page 22).

STEP 2

As your arms come forward, your head starts to drop down. The shoulders are still low.

STEP 3

Your arms reach the front of your stroke as your head drops down again.

STEP 4

Your arms enter the water thumbs first and shoulder width apart. Breathe out.

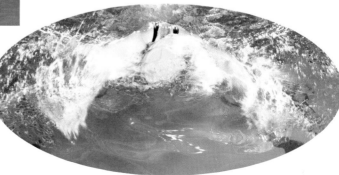

The underwater stroke for the advanced butterfly is similar to freestyle. Your hands drift out a little, make an S-shaped motion as they move under your body, and move back out to finish the stroke.

STEP 1

Your arms drive forward after the two-arm recovery, then swing out to shoulder width apart.

STEP 2

Your arms sweep out a little and then in toward the center line to create an S-shape movement.

STEP 3

As your arms power back, your chin begins to lift.

STEP 4

Lift your chin and take a breath as your arms emerge.

STEP 5

As your arms swing forward, your chin starts to drop.

STEP 6

Your arms come forward and enter the water at the same time as your face does.

LEARNING TO DIVE

*L*earning to dive is great fun, but always make sure that you are in water that is deep enough for diving. Check that there's a lifeguard on duty to help in case you get into trouble. When you start learning, don't worry about how far from the wall you can dive. The main thing is to make as little splash as possible when you enter the water.

STARTER DIVE　　This dive is a good way to get the feeling of going smoothly into the water, instead of making a big splash.

STEP 1
Stand up straight with your arms up and your toes curled over the edge of the pool.

STEP 2
Lean forward, lifting one of your legs up straight behind you. You should aim to be in a straight line from the tips of your fingers to the big toe of your raised leg.

STEP 3
Continue falling forward into the water.

STEP 4
As your body goes into the water, start to bring your legs together.

STEP 5
Try to get your legs together and pointing upward before they disappear in the water.

Once you have got the feeling of going into the water smoothly, try this dive. Don't try to leap out as far as you possibly can. Just try to dive in with as little splash as possible.

STEP 1
Stand on the side of the pool with your arms out in front and your legs slightly bent.

STEP 2
Give a little push off with your feet and let yourself fall forward. Aim to hit a particular spot on the water's surface with your hands.

STEP 3
As your hands go into the water, start to lift your legs up and drop your hips slightly.

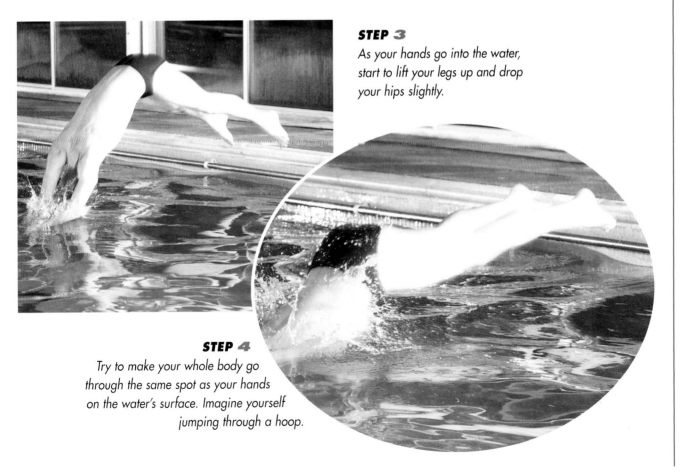

STEP 4
Try to make your whole body go through the same spot as your hands on the water's surface. Imagine yourself jumping through a hoop.

RACING STARTS

In a race, starts and turns are what separate the fastest swimmers from the rest. A good start is important, because it immediately puts you ahead of everyone else. It also makes it less likely that your stroke will be disturbed by waves caused by other swimmers. Practice often to figure out the best angle and distance of your starting dive.

STARTING SEQUENCE

In a race, you use this starting sequence for freestyle, breaststroke, and butterfly. With backstroke, you begin in the water.

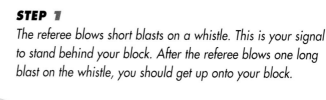

STEP 1
The referee blows short blasts on a whistle. This is your signal to stand behind your block. After the referee blows one long blast on the whistle, you should get up onto your block.

STEP 2
Lean forward to begin the starting position. At this point, it is important to concentrate and stay focused on what you are about to do.

STEP 3
When the starter says "Take your marks!" get into the starting position, ready to dive in. The starter then sets off a starting gun or a loud electronic signal. This is your sign to go!

THE PERFECT DIVE

Diving out a long way from the block isn't necessarily a good dive. Try to make your dive as smooth as possible.

STEP 1
Dive forward, but only to the farthest point that you can comfortably reach.

STEP 2
Start to point your arms and head down toward the water. It might help at first to imagine yourself diving out and over something.

STEP 3
Your arms enter the water with your body straight.

STEP 4
As your hips go into the water, arch your back a little. The moment when you arch your back will determine how deep you go. If you arch it later, you will do a deeper dive.

STEP 5
Glide underwater. Start your stroke only when you feel yourself beginning to slow down.

TOP TIP
Always make sure that the water you are diving into is deep enough that you don't hit the bottom.

RACING TURNS

You must turn at the end of the lane. Perfecting your turns increases your overall speed. You use the power from the momentum of your stroke to perform this twisting, tumbling action.

FREESTYLE TURN (TUMBLE TURN)

The freestyle turn is also called the "tumble turn". It is much faster than just touching the wall and pushing off again is. Start your rotation about 3-4 feet (1–1.5 m) before you reach the wall. It is important to time your stretch so that your feet are able to push off of the wall and back down the lane.

STEP 1
When you are about one stroke away from the wall, drop your hands and shoulders down. Lead with your head, and the rest of your body will follow.

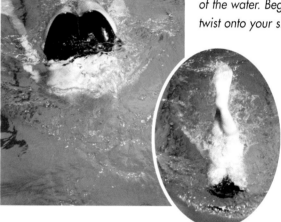

STEP 2
As your body tumbles around, your legs start to rise out of the water. Begin to twist onto your side.

STEP 3
Your feet should hit the wall while you are still on your side. Continue to twist around as you start to push off from the wall.

STEP 4
As you push away from the wall, finish twisting around so that you are on your front. Streamline your body by fully extending your arms and legs.

The turn for these strokes is similar, except that the butterfly is done nearer the surface of the water. In both turns, your hands must hit the wall level and at exactly the same moment.

STEP 1

Hit the wall with your hands together.

STEP 2

Pull one of your shoulders backward—if you are right handed, your right shoulder will probably be most comfortable, and vice versa. At the same time, your legs come in under your body.

STEP 3

Bring your other arm over so that both arms are out in front, ready for you to push off.

BUTTERFLY PUSH OFF

Position yourself on your front before pushing off from the wall to continue your stroke.

BREASTSTROKE PUSH OFF

In breaststroke, you can do one full stroke underwater before coming up for air. Once you have pushed off, pull through underwater. Try to get a really big pull-through, and then glide along with your arms down by your sides.

As you feel that you are about to slow down, bring your hands back through underneath your body and get ready for your kick to the surface. Just as you reach the surface, you can make your armstroke and take a breath!

BACKSTROKE STARTS & TURNS

Backstroke starts and turns are harder to learn, because you can't always see where you're heading while swimming. Recently, swimming laws changed to make backstroke turns easier and faster. The new-style turns are easier for non-racers, as well.

BACKSTROKE START

The starting sequence for the backstroke is slightly different from the other strokes, because you have to start in the water.

STEP 1

The referee blows short blasts on the whistle. This is your signal to jump into the water. Then comes one long blast on the whistle. Swimmers must hold onto either the block or railings with their feet flat against the wall.

STEP 2

The starter says, "Take your marks!". Pull yourself up, ready to go. Your feet should be high, but your toes remain under the water.

STEP 3

"Bang!" You're off! Leap away from the wall, and stretch out as far as you can, with your arms out above your head.

BACKSTROKE TURN

The backstroke turn is a slight variation on the freestyle turn. Use the backstroke flags (see page 5) to work out how far away from the wall you should turn. You will probably need to be four strokes from the wall.

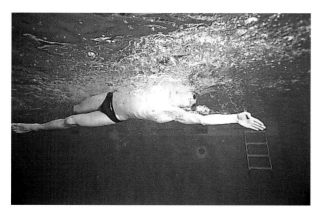

STEP 1

As you get close to the wall, start to turn onto your front. Don't turn over too far from the wall, or you'll end up having to drift in toward it.

STEP 2

Once you are on your front, pull underwater as part of your turn.

STEP 4

Do a tumble turn. The first part of this turn is the same as for freestyle (see page 32), but you do not turn onto your front as your legs hit the wall.

STEP 3

As your arm goes underneath you, propel your body forward to begin the turn.

STEP 5

Push off on your back and reach for the surface, ready for the next length.

TOP TIP

Some backstroke swimmers do butterfly kicks under water after their turns to help them go farther before they come back to the surface.

DIET

Good diet is important for everyone, not just swimmers. But competitive swimmers need to eat a lot of food in order to complete their rigorous training schedules. They often practice several hours a day. While an average person should eat about 1,500–2,000 calories a day, swimmers sometimes eat up to four times this much.

NUTRITION

This diagram shows the percentage of food groups that should be eaten to maintain a balanced diet.

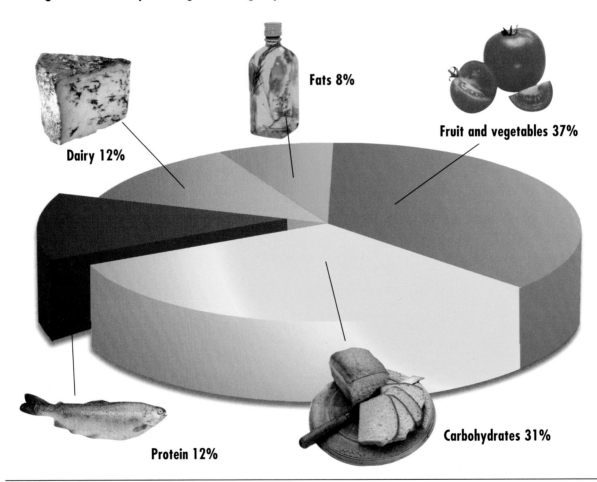

Fats 8%

Fruit and vegetables 37%

Dairy 12%

Carbohydrates 31%

Protein 12%

ENERGY BOOSTERS

If you are doing a lot of exercise, then you need to cut down on fatty foods, and eat plenty of carbohydrates to provide the energy for the exercise that you are doing.

Protein is required for the growth and repair of the body. Try to choose low-fat sources of protein.

TOP TIP
Don't eat fatty foods in the 24 hours before a competition. They are slow to digest, and sit in your stomach for a long time.

FITNESS

Preparing yourself for a race means running through it in your mind beforehand. Block out all other distractions to get yourself 100 per cent focused. Flexibility is crucial for helping you relax and taking your mind off the pressure. It will also help prevent injury. Above all, work on keeping a high level of mental and physical fitness.

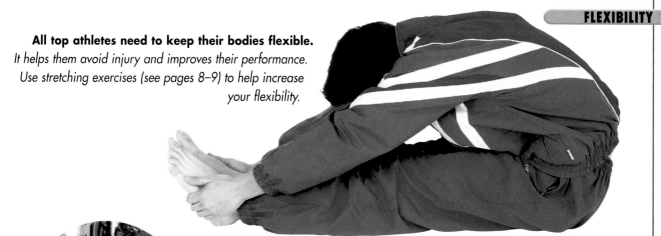

FLEXIBILITY

All top athletes need to keep their bodies flexible.
It helps them avoid injury and improves their performance. Use stretching exercises (see pages 8–9) to help increase your flexibility.

FIT FOR THE TOP

Most professional swimmers do other sports to give them all-around strength.
Anything that keeps you fit and active can make a good break from swimming training. Cycling, tennis, and running are all good activities.

MENTAL ATTITUDE

Winning requires more than just physical strength.
Spend a little time before a race thinking about your starts, turns, and tactics. Don't be distracted by other people. Just concentrate on your own race.

TOP TIP
Don't do too much flexibility work—about 15 minutes every other day is enough.

RACE TACTICS & EVENTS

One of the most important things when competing is that you swim the way that suits you best, instead of matching what other racers are doing. Here are a few hints on how to plan a race of 100 meters or more. Shorter races are pretty much full speed all the way!

COMPETITION RACING

STARTING
Start off fast, at about 95 per cent effort. Your excitement will carry you through the first part of the race quicker than you think.

IN THE MIDDLE
The middle part of the race—lengths two and three of a four-length race, for example—is the most important. Swimmers often ease off a little to save some energy for the last length.

THE TURN
Work hard on your turns to gain ground during the race. The turns are not a time to relax!

STAY AHEAD

Even if you are way ahead, put everything into the last length. There might be someone you haven't spotted very close behind. It might help you to imagine that there's a shark chasing you down the pool!

THE FINISH

Always time your strokes so that you swim hard right up to the wall, instead of drifting in. Races are often won by only a few milliseconds, so every little bit counts!

If you do your best time ever, it doesn't matter whether you come first or last. You're improving, having fun, and doing a healthy sport.

INDIVIDUAL EVENTS

These are the events that are featured in many international competitions.
The rules are set by the Fédération Internationale de Natation Amateur (FINA).

m = meters
- *Freestyle – 50 m, 100 m, 200 m, 400 m, 800 m, 1500 m.*
- *Backstroke – 50 m, 100 m, 200 m.*
- *Breaststroke – 50 m, 100 m, 200 m.*
- *Butterfly – 50 m, 100 m, 200 m.*
- *Individual Medley (all four strokes swum in the order of butterfly, backstroke, breaststroke, freestyle): 100 m (in a 25-m-long pool), 200 m, 400 m.*

TOP TIP

Don't keep looking around at the opposition, because it will cost you time. Instead, just focus on the wall at the end of the pool.

SWIMMING IN OTHER SPORTS

Being a good swimmer isn't just useful if you want to enter races in the swimming pool. There are many other sports that require good water skills. Not only can swimming lead to other interests, but it is one of the best ways to keep fit.

SYNCHRONIZED SWIMMING

Synchronized swimming is a combination of swimming and dance. *This sport is usually done as a team. The swimmers use a series of hand and leg movements to perform sequences. The members of the group move in time with each other and music.*

LONG DISTANCE RACES

Some people enter long distance races held in the sea or even in rivers. *Often these races are from one landmark to another, such as between two piers, or across a channel of water.*

DEEP-SEA DIVING

These divers must be able to swim confidently.
Without good skills, they wouldn't be able to move around well on the bottom of the sea, or swim back to their boats if they ended up a long way away from them.

BOARD DIVING

To be a successful diver, you will need a coach.
Each dive is split into three stages: takeoff, flight, and entry. The divers are graded by judges. Marks are awarded for technique, style, and ability.

SURFING AND BODY BOARDING

Surfers and body boarders need to be strong swimmers for two reasons:
First, they need to be able to swim out and past the breaking waves and white water to the area where they can catch waves. Second, they need to be able to swim back to the beach through rough sea if they get separated from their boards.

TRIATHLON & WATER POLO

Triathlon is becoming increasingly popular with people of all ages. It is one of the hardest sports in the world. One of the first triathlons was called the "Iron Man" contest. Another sport that is really good for strong swimmers is water polo. Water polo players must be able to stay afloat for long periods of time, leap up to catch balls, and move quickly through the water.

TRIATHLON EVENT

This triathlon took place at the 2000 Sydney Olympics. The three events in the triathlon are swimming, cycling, and running. These events are continuous and can involve hundreds of people at once.

LEG 1

The first part of the race is a swim. The distances vary from race to race, but a typical swim might be 875 yards (800m). This could be swum in a pool, a river, the sea, or any other stretch of open water.

LEG 2

The racers then strip off their wetsuits and put on cycling shoes. They run to their bikes and take off. A typical ride might be 15.5 miles (25 km) long.

LEG 3

The final stage is a run. The athletes leave their bikes and bike shoes, put on running shoes, and set off. The run may be anywhere between 6–25 miles (10–40 km) long.

To play water polo, you need to be a very good swimmer. The pace is fast and furious, and your feet cannot touch the bottom of the pool! It is a little like soccer, except that it's played in a swimming pool, and you use your hands to pass and shoot. Each team has eleven players, and the aim is to score as many goals as possible.

PLAYERS

Although the team is made up of eleven players, only seven are allowed to play at any one time. Every water polo team needs to have at least one fast sprinting swimmer!

PASSING

You need to be able to rise up out of the water to pass the ball well. If the ball goes out of the pool, a free throw is awarded to the opposition.

SCORING

Goals are scored by throwing the ball into the back of the net. There are four eight-minute periods, with extra time if the score is tied at the end of the game.

WATER SAFETY

Never forget that any water that's deep enough to cover your face can be dangerous. The sea and rivers are especially deadly, and hundreds of people drown in them every year. But even swimming pools with lifeguards on duty see several deaths a year. It's up to you to learn how to play safely in the water.

RIP CURRENTS

These dangerous currents claim many lives each year. They form where waves are breaking. If you are unlucky enough to be caught in one, stay calm, and concentrate on getting out of the current. You can use this same technique to get out of other fast-flowing water currents.

Rip current flows out through deeper water

deep water

Undertow

Undertow

shallow water

STEP 1

Swim across the current. Don't try to swim against it. Struggling too hard will only make you tired.

STEP 2

Once you are safely out of the current, swim calmly back to shore.

If you see the sign on the right it means "Do not swim". A red flag means "danger: do not enter the water". Be sure to obey these warnings, or you will put your own life in danger, as well as the life of the person who may have to rescue you.

Depth markers such as this one tell you in either feet or meters how deep the water is. Never dive into water that is less than 6 feet (2 m) deep, or any water in which there might be an obstruction.

DO

- *Look out for warning signs*
- *Tell someone where you are going*
- *Obey notices and flags telling you where to swim*
- *Swim parallel to the shore, keeping it in sight at all times*
- *Get out of the water if it gets cold*

DON'T

- *Swim alone*
- *Swim near piers or in areas with strong currents*
- *Swim near boats or other water vessels*
- *Go out of your depth if you are not a good swimmer*
- *Dive into water that is less than 6 feet (2 m) deep; you can seriously injure yourself*

WARNING

If you're not sure that you can cope with the conditions, don't go into the sea. Surfers have a saying about this: "If in doubt, don't go out."

LIFESAVING

Learning the basic skills of lifesaving could one day save your life or the life of someone else. Most water safety is common sense, but water is dangerous if it is not respected. Remember that play can turn into something much more serious in a matter of seconds.

RIVER RESCUE

It's very dangerous to wade into a fast-flowing river to rescue someone clinging to a rock or log. This is probably the least dangerous way to do it, if there are enough people.

STEP 1
The first person in the group wades out a little way, holding hands with the next person.

STEP 2
Each person in the group steps into the water holding hands with the person in front and behind.

STEP 3
Eventually, they form a chain of people angled slightly downstream. The person farthest out in the river may be able to make a rescue.

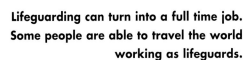

The key to rescuing someone is to be sure that you are safe, as well as the person in trouble. Details of basic lifesaving courses are available from your local swimming clubs.

This swimmer is practicing towing someone who needs rescuing. The rescuer is keeping the person's head above water so he has a chance to breathe.

Lifeguarding can turn into a full time job. Some people are able to travel the world working as lifeguards.
Even if you don't want to work as a lifeguard, it's a very useful skill to have. If you spot someone in the water who is in trouble, you will be able to help him or her.

... YOU ARE IN TROUBLE

- *Stay calm*
- *Be decisive. Either:*
  - *– float until someone arrives*
  - *– tread water and wave one arm for assistance*
  - *– if you swim back to safety, use the backstroke, but with the breaststroke leg action to move faster. Being on your back keeps your head out of water, and allows you to breathe more easily*

... SOMEONE ELSE IS IN TROUBLE

- *Stay calm*
- *Shout for help, or go and get help from someone else*
- *Do not go into the water to help if you don't have lifesaving training*
- *Use objects such as life preservers to rescue the person without swimming toward them. Otherwise, you could both end up in trouble!*

HOW THE PROS DO IT

Being a competitive swimmer is very hard work. Few people get rich in this sport—even the best swimmers struggle to make a living. Only Olympic gold medalists are able to earn large amounts of money from product endorsements and media interviews. As with most athletes, competitive swimmers take part in the sport because they love it.

TRAINING DIARY

6:00	*Wake up. Drink a cup of tea, fruit juice or water.*
6:30 – 8:30	*Training in the pool.*
9:00 – 11:30	*Eat breakfast: lots of carbohydrates, such as bread and jam, cereal, and scrambled eggs.*
12:00 – 1:00	*Flexibility session, gym work or swim-bench training.*
1:30	*Eat lunch—the biggest meal of the day: more carbohydrates, such as pasta, bread and rice, but also protein (meat or fish) and vegetables.*
5:30 – 7:00	*Training in the pool.*
8:00	*Go home and rest.*
10:00	*Bedtime.*

And the next day it starts all over again...

MONEY

Alexander Popov, a Russian swimmer, has been one of the world's best for over a decade.
Popov is one of the few people to make money from swimming. Even people who make it to the Olympic finals sometimes struggle to fund their swimming.

IAN THORPE "THORPEDO"

Ian Thorpe won several gold medals at the 2000 Olympics.
The most thrilling was the last stage of the men's 4 x 100m freestyle, in which Thorpe's Australian team beat the United States by a narrow margin. Thorpe overtook the American 100m specialist Gary Hall Jr. in the last few strokes to snatch gold.

Janet Evans is one of the United States' most successful female swimmers.

To win Olympic gold medals, you have to work extremely hard. Even the best swimmers in the world don't win without training every day. There are lots of talented swimmers in the world. The ones who train the hardest often win the gold medals.

There are swimming clubs across the world that regularly hold national competitions, galas, and international championships. This is a typical day for a swimmer in an inter-club gala.

6:00	*Wake up thinking you have to go training. Remember it's a race day and go back to sleep.*
9:00	*Get up: have some breakfast (not as much as usual), and drink plenty of juice or water. Avoid drinking too much tea or coffee.*
9:30 – 12:00	*Rest, maybe do a little flexibility work.*
12:30	*Eat a light lunch with lots of carbohydrates: avoid meat, cheese, and fatty foods.*
3:00	*Travel to the gala.*
5:00	*Warm up.*
5:30	*The gala starts: swimmers wait for their races.*
8:30	*The gala finishes: go home and reflect on the high and low points of the race for next time.*

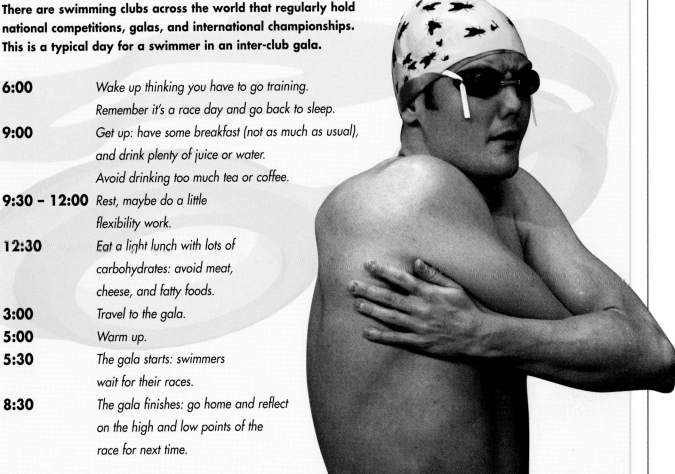

TOP TIP
Everyone on a team should cheer for one another. Cheering helps each swimmer on your team do better in their races, including yourself!

GLOSSARY

ARMSTROKE – The action of your arms while swimming.

DOLPHIN KICK – The leg action used for the butterfly stroke.

DRAG – Resistance in the water caused by clothing and hair.

FREE START – When someone dives in before the gun has signaled the start of the race, it is called a "false start". This will result in disqualification.

GALA – A set of swimming races taking place one after another.

GLIDE – The use of momentum to move through the water before starting a stroke. Arms are held against the body, with legs out to the back for a streamlined action.

KICK BOARD – A float that you hold on to while swimming with your legs only.

OLYMPICS – A sporting competition held every four years, where the best of the world's sportspeople, from many different sports, take part.

OVERARM RECOVERY – The part of your armstroke that takes place above water.

PULL BUOY – A float that you tuck between your thighs to help you stay in the right position in the water when swimming with your arms only.

PULL – The part of your armstroke that moves you forward through the water.

RECOVERY – The point at which the arms or legs return to the starting position.

STARTING BLOCK – A small, raised platform from which racing swimmers dive at the start of a race.

TRIATHLON – A race made up of swimming, cycling, and running events.

TRICKLE BREATHING – Releasing air in short bursts when under water.

TUMBLE TURN – A freestyle turn where your hands don't touch the wall. Instead, you duck down under water and flip your feet over to hit the wall, then push off for your next length.

TWO-ARM RECOVERY – The term given to the action of the arms above water during the butterfly stroke.

UNDERWATER STROKE – See pull.

INDEX

B

backstroke 5, 14-17
  start 4, 28, 32
  turn 32, 33
body boarding 39
breaststroke 4, 18-21
  finish 31
  start 28
  turn 31
breathing 10, 15, 18, 23, 24
butterfly 4, 22-5
  finish 31
  start 28
  turn 31, 33

C

clothing 6, 7

D

deep-sea diving 39
diet 34
diving 26-9, 39

E

equipment 6, 7
Evans, Janet 47
events 37

F

Féderation Internationale de Natation Amateur (FINA) 37
fitness 35
flags 5, 33
freestyle 4, 10-13
  start 28
  turn 30

L

lifesaving 44, 45

O

Olympic medalists 46, 47

P

Popov, Alexander 46

R

racing
  long distance 38
  starts 4, 5, 28, 29
  tactics 36, 37
  turns 30, 31

S

safety 42-5
starts 5, 26-9, 32, 33, 36
strokes 8-23
  see also individual strokes
surfing 39
swimming pools 4, 5
synchronized swimming 38

T

Thorpe, Ian 46
triathlon 40
tumble turns 30, 33
turns 28-33, 36

W

warming up 8, 9
water polo 40, 41
water safety 42, 43

Printed in the USA